Octave Chanute

America's Expert on Flight

by Barbara A. Donovan

SCHOOL PUBLISHERS

Cover, Baldwin H. Ward & Kathryn C. Ward/Corbis; 3, Science Museum/SSPL/The Image Works; 4, The Granger Collecion/New York; 5, LL/Roger Viollet/Getty Images; 6, Minnesota Historical Society/Corbis; 7, Science Museum, London/Topham-HIP/The Image Works; 8, Hulton Archive/Getty Images; 9, Library of Congress; 10, Hulton Archive/Getty Images; 11, Hulton Archive/Getty Images; 12, C.P. Cushing/ClassicStock.com; 12 May Evans Picture Library/Alamy; 13, RobertStock.com; 14, National Aviation Museum/Corbis.

Printed in China

ISBN 10: 0-15-350303-3
ISBN 13: 978-0-15-350303-0

Ordering Options
ISBN 10: 0-15-349941-9 (Grade 6 ELL Collection)
ISBN 13: 978-0-15-349941-8 (Grade 6 ELL Collection)
ISBN 10: 0-15-357344-9 (package of 5)
ISBN 13: 978-0-15-357344-6 (package of 5)

5 6 7 8 9 10   0940   12 11 10 09

The Wright brothers were not the first to become interested in flight. Inventors had been trying to build machines that could fly for many years before anyone succeeded. Some inventors built models. Other inventors tried to build flying machines that could carry a person. There were many ideas and designs. Some ideas worked. Others did not.

One problem for inventors was that it was difficult to find out what others had tried. A man named Octave Chanute was very smart and organized. He pulled together as much information about flight as he could because he thought flying was very interesting. If people had questions about flying machines, they turned to Octave Chanute.

The Engineer

Octave Chanute was born in Paris in 1832. He moved to the United States when he was six years old. Young Chanute decided to become an engineer. An engineer is someone who uses science to design or build things, such as buildings, bridges, or airplanes.

When Chanute was seventeen, he wanted a job at the Hudson River Railroad. At first, the people at the railroad did not want to hire him. He did not give up. He said he would work for free if they would let him work there. They agreed.

Chanute started out holding the chain for the people studying the land for the railroad. It was a very low job. Still, he did it happily. Chanute was smart and worked hard. He learned all he could about the railroad. Soon he became an engineer. He held more important jobs.

When he was thirty-five years old, he took on one of the most difficult engineering jobs. He was in charge of building the first bridge across the mighty Missouri River. The bridge was finished in 1869. Chanute was now a respected engineer.

From 1869 until 1885, Chanute was very busy. He was the engineer on many important jobs. During this time, he began to read some articles about flying machines that he found very interesting. However, he decided to put them aside for the time being. He had work to do.

The Problem Solver

In 1885, Chanute retired from his engineering job. He had become interested in the idea of how to stop wood from rotting. The country needed wood for new telephone poles and railroad ties. Chanute found a solution to that problem. He discovered that a kind of sticky tar would keep the wood from rotting. This discovery led to a successful business for him.

The Author

By 1890, Chanute's business was doing so well that he had time to relax. Now he had time for the idea that had interested him years before—flight. Chanute read every article he could find on the subject. He bought books on flight. He borrowed books from libraries. He

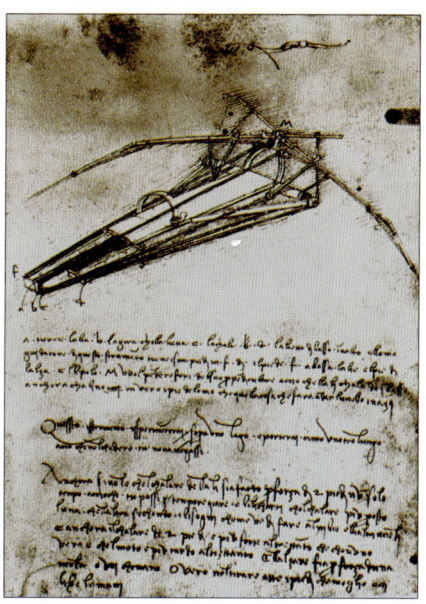

wrote letters to inventors who were working on flying machines. He sponsored meetings. At these meetings, people interested in flight could share what they knew.

In 1891, Chanute started writing articles for a magazine. By 1894, he had written enough articles for a book. He called his book *Progress in Flying Machines*. It became the most important book for inventors interested in flight. That is because the book contained most everything that people had ever discovered about flight. In the book, Chanute described what had worked. He also discussed what hadn't worked and why.

Chanute 1896. Ailes multiples Second modèle, genam- ayant le biplan.

The Idea Tester

Around that same time, Chanute decided he was ready to test his own ideas about flight. He hired some young inventors to help him build his flying machines. He was always helping young inventors. They would help him now.

In 1895, Chanute began building flying machines. The following year, he invited Augustus Moore Herring to join him and some workers in Chicago. Herring had been testing his own flying machines called gliders. Gliders are like airplanes without engines. Herring agreed to help Chanute in Chicago.

Chanute was building gliders, too. Chanute's first design had many wings. It had so many wings that it looked like an insect. For this reason, workers called it the "Katydid." A katydid is a kind of grasshopper. On June 22, 1896, Chanute's glider was ready. A worker climbed in and took off. The flying machine only went a little way, but it flew!

Chanute was testing his machines on the shore of Lake Michigan. He was in a spot far away from others. He did not want anyone to know about his flying machines. Still, someone had noticed the glider flight. The next day, a newspaper reporter showed up. Before long, crowds of reporters arrived to report on the test flights. Chanute and his gliders were famous.

Herring also flew the glider for Chanute in some test flights. Herring built another glider, too. It had a tail that was in the shape of a cross. The tail could move. It worked to stabilize the glider so that it could fly better.

Chanute liked that idea. He decided to build a glider with a tail that moved. He also used ideas from his work building bridges to build his glider.

Chanute's new glider had three wings. It also had a tail that moved. He discovered that the three wings made the glider too hard to handle. It was not safe. Chanute took off the bottom wing. Now he had a biplane—a glider with two wings, one above the other.

It worked! After a few days, Herring and the others could fly the glider for distances greater than 300 feet (91 m). Chanute had taken an important step toward inventing an airplane.

The Flight Expert

Many inventors wrote to Chanute over the years. In May of 1900, he got a letter from Wilbur Wright. He told Chanute that he and his brother planned to build a glider much like the one Chanute and Herring had built. Wright also asked Chanute for ideas on the best place to test his glider.

Chanute explained that he had done well testing his flying machines along Lake Michigan. Good winds blew by the water's edge. The sand made a soft place to land the glider. Chanute suggested a few similar places that might work.

For many years after that, Wilbur Wright and Chanute wrote letters back and forth. They told each other what they had tried and learned. Chanute also visited the Wright brothers. He went to Kitty Hawk, North Carolina, as they tested their flying machines.

Chanute was many things during his life. He was an engineer. He ran a business. He was a writer. He was an inventor. Most of all, he was a friend to other inventors. He believed strongly in sharing experiences. In that way, everyone learned from what went right or wrong. Octave Chanute was an important part of the early history of flight.

Scaffolded Language Development

TIME PHRASE Review the following sentence from the selection:

In 1885, Chanute retired from his engineering job. *(page 6)*

Point out that the sentence begins with a phrase that tells the time of the event and that the phrase is followed by a comma. The phrase could also be added to the end of the sentence: *Chanute retired from his engineering job in 1885.* In that case, there is no comma. Remind students that time phrases are useful in determining the sequence of events.

Have students identify the time phrases in the following sentences and then rewrite each sentence with the time phrase at the beginning. Students may check their work by rereading the selection.

1. He took one of the most difficult engineering jobs when he was thirty-five years old.
2. Chanute was very busy from 1869 until 1885.
3. He took a job at the Hudson River Railroad when he was seventeen.
4. He got a letter from Wilbur Wright in May of 1900.
5. Wilbur Wright and Chanute wrote letters back and forth for many years after that.

 Science

Time to Write Have students research other important scientific facts about Chanute and his work. Ask them to compare their list of facts with those of their classmates.

 **School-Home Connection** Encourage students to tell family members about Octave Chanute and how he helped inventors such as the Wright brothers.

Word Count: 1,140